Tailgating without a Hitch

Kathy Clyne Merrill

Proctor Publications • Ann Arbor • Michigan

Copyright © 1996 by Kathy Clyne Merrill

Library of Congress Catalog Card Number: 96–70134

ISBN: 1–882792–32–7

Publisher's Cataloging in Publication
(Prepared by Quality Books, Inc.)
Merrill, Kathy Clyne.
    Tailgating without a hitch / by Kathy Clyne Merrill.
    p. cm.
    Includes index.

    1. Outdoor cookery. 2. Tailgate parties. I. Title.
TX823.M47 1996   641.5'78
                        QBI96-40299

Proctor Publications
P.O. Box 2498
Ann Arbor, Michigan 48106–2498
(800) 343–3034
(313) 480–9900

This book is dedicated to my late father

Alfred P. Clyne

who not only taught me to enjoy a variety
of cuisine but also the love of preparing
such gourmet delights.

Special Thanks

to all of my close friends and family for testing all the various concoctions I have whipped up over the years. Some have been fantastic successes, but some have been the test of true friendship. Immense gratitude to my husband, Rick, for his patience and assistance with my tailgate innovations. Without his support, many of the recipes included in this book would not have become edible realities. Appreciation to Jerilyn Davis for her continuing encouragement and Janet Opdyke for her professional consultation. Last, but not least, special recognition to all of my guinea pigs: my mother, Lorraine Clyne; in-laws, Dick and JoAnn Merrill; friends, Marilyn and Tim Bannon, Sandy Boulton, Molly Resnick and John Martin, Doug and Marji Theodoroff; and fellow Rotarian Gourmet Club members.

CONTENTS

INTRODUCTION

As a graduate of the University of Michigan, I believe that the ritual of a tailgate party is the protocol for every college football event. With a good twenty years of tailgating under my belt, I have observed various tailgate activities, from delivered pizza, submarine sandwiches, and hot dogs and hamburgers on the grill to lavish tables of gourmet fare with candelabras. Coupling my history of Michigan tailgate parties and the love of cooking, I started pleasing my small party of tailgaters with creations of grilled or cooked entrees fixed right in the parking lot. We have had several visitors, some acquaintances and some just tantalized by the aroma, visit our tailgate to discuss the process of fixing the meal at the tailgate location as well as ask for a copy of the recipe. With these requests as incentive, I figured it was time to document this process to share with all of my fellow tailgaters or those of you who just love to cook outdoors.

This book describes recipes and a process that may be utilized at any event where you wish to gather friends together in a dinner party setting. Enough discussion about the motivation behind this publication. Let's get into the tailgate process and get you started preparing the ensuing recipes or creating your own adaptation of your favorite dishes.

SEASON PLANNING

Michigan natives boast or complain about Michigan's fickle weather in that if you do not like the current state of affairs, stick around for awhile and it will change. Michigan's inconsistent weather provides a challenge to those who prepare for any outdoor event. Therefore, the subsequent section details how to prepare for a season of Michigan football and invariably Michigan's unpredictable weather.

A usual Michigan tailgate season includes six game Saturdays, starting with unseasonably warm weather in late August and ending with bitter cold for the last game of the season late in November. Planning a season with this disparity in weather may be a formidable task, but if you consider the seasonal normal temperatures and are always prepared for inclement weather, you will find your tailgate party a success whether it's sunny or not. For example, a canopy with tent poles to hoist up in the air is handy or you could borrow/rent a large van, depending on the size of the party. The expense of this approach is not necessary though. We have used a large tarp with one tent pole, which we position between two cars. It may be necessary to purchase three parking spaces to accomplish this, depending on where you park. We use the car doors to fasten down the tarp on the sides and use the pole in the middle for height. Amazingly, we have only had to resort to this practice for one game during the last ten years when it "poured" during the whole tailgate party: Michigan vs. Notre Dame, 1989. We also stock our vehicle with inexpensive plastic ponchos for those tailgate folks not adequately prepared for rain. A list of equipment is included, defining both inexpensive and expensive measures to take for your tailgating pleasure, later in this book.

To get started with planning your tailgate parties for the season, the following diagram describes the type of menus you may want to pursue, capitalizing on typical weather conditions. More detailed recipes are provided for each entry in the recipe section.

Weather Conditions	Main Entree
Warm weather brunch Plan a minimum 2 hours for tailgate (early game).	Pancakes and Sausage Skillet Frittata with Italian sausage Sake Marinated Grilled Shrimp with bagels and assorted toppings
Warm weather lunch Plan a minimum 2 hours for tailgate (early game).	Mixed Sausages in Beer Lamb Burgers Sausage, Apple, and Onion Shish Kebab Barbecued Ribs and/or Chicken

Weather Conditions	Main Entree
Moderately warm or cold weather lunch or dinner Plan a minimum 3 hours for tailgate (early or late afternoon game).	Paella Teriyaki Salmon Grilled, Rolled and Stuffed Turkey Breast Grilled, Glazed Corned Beef with Mother-in-Law's Beans Pork Roast with Orange Mustard Sauce and baked apples Shashlyk Iz Baraniny (Lamb Shish Kebab)
End of season super cold weather lunch Plan a minimum 2 hours for tailgate.	Grilled Jerk Chicken Crushed Buckeye Chili

POTLUCK STRATEGY

Many of your guests will want to contribute to your tailgate party. At least you hope they will since your hands
will be full preparing the entree. It has been my experi-
ence that our invited guests are more than happy to bring
an accompaniment for the tailgate meal. Remember to
tell your fellow tailgaters how many people will be at
your party so they will bring enough servings to feed the
crowd. Listed below are some suggestions.

Appetizers

This course will depend on how long you plan to munch
before the entree is ready to be served. We usually have
at least two appetizers along with raw vegetables with a
dip for eight to ten tailgaters. This will help assuage your
hungry tailgaters until the entree is ready.

- Crackers and cheese
- Assorted nuts
- Raw vegetables and dip
- Tortilla chips with salsa
- Pretzels or flavored pretzel chips
- Cinnamon rolls or assorted pastries
- Bagels with assorted toppings (cream cheese,
  chopped onion, tomatoes and olives, lox,
  small shrimp, caviar)
- Hot spiced wine or cider

Salads

The warmer tailgate parties welcome a salad, whereas for the colder games we resort to a hot side dish.

- Tossed greens with light dressing (apply dressing at the party)
- Tossed blanched vegetables, such as green beans or broccoli, in light dressing
- Potato, macaroni, or pasta salad
- Cole slaw or shredded carrot salad
- Mixed fruits

Bread

Fresh bread is always devoured, especially with Paella or other stews for which the bread is used to soak up the juices left in your bowl or plate. Flavored butters are always fun when you use minced fresh herbs, onion, and/or garlic blended well with soft butter. Prepare this a couple days ahead so the flavors blend well.

- Bread sticks, soft or crunchy
- Italian or French bread with assorted flavored butters
- Croissants or biscuits
- Corn bread
- Naan or flat bread
- Bagels
- Cinnamon rolls or other pastries

Side Dishes

Some of the items listed below require preparation the morning of the tailgate because they will need to be warmed up and then wrapped in a "cooler" type container, insulated to keep the dish hot, or wrapped in several layers of newspaper. Baked potatoes are also an option when you microwave them in the morning and then wrap them in heavy-duty aluminum foil and newspaper to keep warm. We also have a hot plate or propane burner and grill available, when appropriate, for those who wish to warm the item up in the pot at the tailgate location.

- Grilled skewered vegetables such as summer squash, onions, and cherry tomatoes
- Baked beans, commercially prepared or Mother-in-Law's Beans
- Baked casserole dish: au gratin potatoes or green beans, for example
- Baked apples (Core, add spices, and wrap in foil to be cooked on the grill for 15 to 25 minutes, depending on how hot your fire is. Poke one with a sharp knife to check for doneness. Apples are especially good with pork chops or grilled pork roast.)

Desserts

I never worry about this portion of the feast. We have a couple of real sweet tooths in our crowd, including my husband, so we always have super finishes to our hearty tailgate party. The ice cream sundae listed below involves packing the ice cream in dry ice. This seems like a lot of trouble, but the effort is well worth the enjoyment of diving into an ice cream delight on a hot football Saturday. We often delay the dessert until after the game since we are usually stuffed from the morning's victuals.

- Cookies or brownies
- Ice cream sundae with assorted toppings
- Apples with peanut butter or caramel dip
- Fruit pies
- Leftover Halloween candy or Girl Scout cookies

Once the entree has been determined, you will need to coordinate the accompaniments as a complement to your theme. Offer suggestions to your tailgate participants or tell them what the entree is and let them be creative with their offerings. Also, plan your assignments according to the culinary capabilities of your tailgate participants. We find that the stress of participating in our party is lessened if we assign a bag of tortilla chips with a jar of salsa or a can of nuts to the singleton who does not like to cook, a more elaborate side dish or salad to the tailgater who loves to cook, the bread to one who lives close to a great bakery or has a bread machine, and dessert to the sweet lover or to those planning to arrive late to the game.

Last, but not least, we ask our fellow tailgaters to bring their own liquid libations. Our parties usually include coffee for the early morning kick start, as well as wine, beer, and various sodas and water. Hot spiced wine or cider and hot chocolate are perfect for the colder season. Everyone brings their favorite, which always turns out to be more than adequate. If you plan an extremely large tailgate party and do not have enough food assignments for everyone, you might ask folks to bring a bottle of wine, champagne, spiced rum, or Bailey's to add to coffee or hot chocolate.

GRILLING PROCEDURE

Setting up your grill requires a survey of the area in which you plan to tailgate. Please try to select a site where you can place your grill away from your fellow tailgaters as well as surrounding tailgaters. Nothing is more disturbing than to have a grilling tailgater channeling smoke, albeit unintentionally, through your tailgate party. So please be respectful by selecting a tailgate site where you can position your grill away from fellow tailgate participants and other tailgate parties. We have selected a site where we can set up our grill on a street or drive, away from picnicking tailgaters. With this setup, we do not worry about the direction of our smoke, especially with an entree that requires more than 15 minutes to cook.

Several of the recipes rely on three different grilling set-ups:

- Charcoal or Gas, Direct Method
- Charcoal, Indirect Method
- Charcoal and Wood, Direct Method

The following section provides general descriptions of each process. Check the manufacturer's instructions for more specific guidance.

Charcoal, Direct Method

The direct method of grilling includes charcoal spread evenly across the charcoal rack of the grill or a traditional

11

gas grill cooking surface. The entree is placed directly above the heat source and must be turned to expose both sides of the entree to the heat. This method is primarily used when the entree is cooked quickly in 5 to 25 minutes.

To set up a charcoal grill in this fashion, remove the grilling rack from the grill to expose the lower rack, which holds the charcoal. Open all dampers. Crumple a piece of newspaper and place it on the lower rack. Add charcoal to the lower grill, covering the newspaper. The number of briquettes depends on the amount of cooking time you need for your entree. Thirty briquettes is a basic rule of thumb for the quickest entrees. Again, your manufacturer's instructions may be the best guide to the amount of charcoal.

Mound up the briquettes on the lower rack on top of the newspaper. Spray the charcoal with lighter fluid if the briquettes are not self-lighting. Ignite the charcoal and let it burn for 25 to 30 minutes until the charcoal is covered with a light gray ash and is no longer flaming. Spread the charcoal evenly across the lower rack and place the grilling rack onto the grill. Let the grilling rack heat up before adding the entree unless you are cooking in a roast rack or heavy-duty aluminum foil. If cooking directly on the grill rack, spray the rack with cooking oil spray or other oil. Then feel free to add your entree right away. Place the cover on the grill if you are cooking on a roast rack or in heavy-duty aluminum foil packets.

Gas, Direct Method

With gas grilling, open the lid. Check that all burner control knobs are turned to 'Off' and that the fuel scale reads more than 'E.' Next turn the gas on at the source (turn the LP tank valve to 'On'). Light the grill according to the manufacturer's directions, with the igniter switch or a match if necessary. Close the lid and preheat the barbecue until the thermometer registers 500 to 550 degrees Fahrenheit (260 to 288 degrees Centigrade). This will take 10 to 15 minutes. To cook, adjust burner controls as the recipe directs.

Charcoal, Indirect Method

This method is used for larger cuts of meat and other foods that require a longer cooking time. Foods are cooked by reflected heat, like in a convection oven. This insures faster cooking and juicier meats without turning. This method can only be used with a covered or kettle grill. Indirect cooking is a no-peek method. In fact, every time you lift the grill lid, heat escapes, increasing your grilling time. The food is not placed directly above the heat, so there is no need for frequent checking. Because heat circulates around the food, much like in a convection oven, you do not need to turn foods when they are cooked by the indirect method.

To set up your grill for the indirect method, remove the grill lid and open all dampers. Arrange an equal number of briquettes on each side of the lower grate. As in the direct charcoal method, spray the charcoal with lighter fluid and ignite. The briquettes are ready when covered with a light gray ash, about 30 minutes. Make sure the coals are burning equally well on both sides before beginning to cook. Place a heavy-duty aluminum foil drip pan in the center of the lower grate between the coals or on the top rack if using a roast rack. (We have also set up the grill in the "direct method" when placing the drip pan and roast rack on the top grill.) Position the cooking grate with handles over the coals, so additional briquettes may be added to each side every hour. Food should be placed on the cooking grate above the drip pan. Place the lid on the grill and cook as the recipe directs.

EQUIPMENT – THE BASICS

The equipment described in this section is itemized in the following recipes. Each recipe includes a list of equipment necessary to execute the recipe at your tailgate site. This list provides you with an idea of the general equipment necessary, most of which you will find in your inventory of cooking accessories at home. The items listed in the last three categories (eating utensils, cleaning supplies, and other essentials) will most likely be necessary for every game. We have a picnic basket equipped with many of the mainstay supplies on hand for the entire tailgate season.

The kettle grill we use is a full size grill, retrofitted by my husband with the short legs from our portable grill. This renovation was necessary to provide enough grilling space for the large cuts of meat we often serve to our large party of tailgaters. If your tailgate parties consist of four to six folks, a portable kettle grill may be sufficient. You may want to cut the entree into smaller portions adequate to fit on a smaller grill and then grill in stages.

You will also note that in many of the recipes I use a tremendous amount of disposable items, like heavy-duty aluminum foil, paper towels, disposable plates, cups, and plastic bags. This approach is not the most environmentally sound; the purpose of the disposable items is to minimize the amount of cleanup conducted during and as you wrap up your tailgate party. This is especially important when the tailgate party bumps into the kickoff of a game. This strategy also reduces the amount of washing needed at home after a long day of tailgating. Each entree in the recipe section lists the required equipment to accomplish the task.

Cooking Devices

- Portable kettle grill with charcoal and igniter
- Gas grill
- Cookplate or cookstove (propane)

Cooking Tools

- Grilling or long-handled fork
- Grilling or long-handled tongs
- Long-handled spatula
- Long-handled ladle
- Grilling insulated mitts
- Metal or bamboo skewers
- Aluminum drip pan and roast rack
- Heavy-duty, extra-wide aluminum foil
- Meat thermometer
- Large plastic or wooden cutting board
- Sharp butcher or carving knife

Processing Containers

- Freezer zipper-style plastic bags
- Various sizes of mixing bowls
- Large stock pot
- Saucepan

Eating Utensils

- Paper or plastic plates (We prefer plastic for sturdiness – pick your favorite color. Ours is maize and blue.)
- Paper or plastic bowls (Again, we favor plastic for sturdiness, as well as a large serving size for the stews.)
- Plastic silverware (We have heavy-duty maize and blue plastic flatware that we recycle in the dishwasher.)
- Styrofoam or plastic glasses (obviously, color-coordinated in a favorite hue.)
- Appetizer- and dinner-size paper napkins

Cleaning Supplies

- Paper towels
- Premoistened towels, such as Wet Ones, for messy finger foods or preparation
- Plastic garbage bags to collect trash

Other Essentials

- Insulated containers for cooling liquid re-freshments, storing chilled items, and keeping baked dishes warm. To help keep dishes warm, wrap the dish in newspaper and place it in a cooler or insulated container. If a cooler is not available, wrap the dish in newspaper and then a blanket.

- Large jug of water for extinguishing the coals or rinsing dishes before storing them away after the tailgate. Recycled large, plastic milk jugs work well.
- Plastic garbage bag for refuse if a trash container is not available near your tailgate site.
- Salt and pepper
- Sugar or sugar substitute (Small bags are convenient.)

TAILGATE RECIPE
CONVERSION PROCESS

This section describes how to convert your recipes for a tailgate party. Most recipes may be converted into a tailgate entree. There are just a few simple rules to follow.

- Perform as much prep work as possible the night before or a day ahead of your tailgate party.

- If you marinate meat or poultry, limit the time the food is marinating to 24 hours at most, especially if the marinade consists of an acid base. The acid content might be wine, vinegar or fruit juice.

- Put the meat and marinade in a freezer-style bag and place it in the refrigerator until the morning of the tailgate. Wrap the food in foil at home before the tailgate if you plan to use foil packets for cooking.

- Premix and measure in separate plastic bags dry and wet ingredients. This step provides you with the ability to simply pour the liquid into the dry ingredients and massage the bag to blend them at your tailgate site.

- Prepare vegetables or fruit at home the night before or morning of the tailgate. Clean, slice, or chop, whatever your recipe instructs, and place in plastic bags so that all you have to do is pour the items into your pot or pan at the tailgate party. Squeeze fresh lemon juice over fruit if you prepare your dish the night before. The lemon juice will help the fruit stay fresh and reduce discoloration.

19

- Remember to bring your meat or poultry to room temperature before grilling so that it will cook evenly. Also, if you need to chill your food traveling to your tailgate party, let it sit someplace at a moderate temperature, mid-60 to mid-70 degrees if possible, for an hour before cooking. Obviously, on an extremely cold day, set your entree in the car or in a cooler without ice for the hour before cooking. Even though your car's internal temperature may not be warm enough to raise your main course to 60 to 70 degrees, it will keep it from freezing, which will prolong your cooking time.

- Research the internal temperature your grilled entree should reach for your desired doneness. In the case of a large cut of meat, such as roast beef, whole turkey or roasting chicken, use a meat thermometer to help you decide when to remove your tailgate delight from the grill. Remember to subtract 10 degrees from the desired temperature and take your entree off of the grill when it reaches the revised temperature. Let the meat or poultry sit for 15 to 20 minutes before carving. Cover with heavy-duty aluminum foil to keep warm. The roast or bird will cook the additional 10 degrees while covered with foil. The new instant thermometers are handy when grilling smaller pieces of meat or chicken. Use as directed by the manufacturer.

- Think through your entire recipe for the type of equipment you will need to fully prepare the entree. Writing down the necessary provisions on a piece of paper, a column each for ingredients and equipment, will help you get organized as you read through the recipe. If you do not have the proper equipment to perform all of the tasks at the tailgate site, prepare at home and finish at your tailgate party. This may involve simply reheating on a propane cookstove or cookplate or preparing a dish to the point of baking and then baking it on the kettle grill using the indirect method of cooking.

• If you are grilling with charcoal or wood, make sure you bring along a generous amount of water to put out your fire. Dump the embers onto recycled heavy-duty aluminum foil and drench with water. Fold up the foil with the ash and dispose. If you tailgate at a site allowing you to leave your grill out during the game, this step may be eliminated if the embers are completely extinguished. We still drench them with water just to insure that we will not start a fire in the garbage receptacle where we dispose of our waste. As mentioned in the equipment section, recycled milk jugs work well for this task.

• When using an aluminum foil pan in both the preparation and serving stages of your tailgate party, line the pan with fresh heavy-duty aluminum foil before you put your cooked entree in the pan. Make sure you do not put cooked food in a container that carried raw food, especially chicken or meat. Therefore, lining the pan with fresh heavy-duty aluminum foil will allow you one pan for preparation and serving, with protection from the raw to cooked stage. Use additional heavy-duty aluminum foil to cover the cooked entree to keep it warm for second helpings.

Pasta may be an entree, although patience is required because it is difficult to bring water to a boil on a cookstove or propane cookplate rapidly. You may want to cook pasta at home and then add to hot water at your tailgate site to warm it up. This tactic is facilitated by cooking your pasta to just short of fully cooked; in other words, the pasta may have a slight bite. Drain the pasta and place in a plastic bag. Transport the pasta to your tailgate site. Heat a pot of water on your propane stove, cookplate, or a grill until steaming. Add your cooked pasta and stir occasionally to ensure that the pasta does not stick to the bottom of the pot. Five minutes should be adequate to heat your pasta up and complete the cooking process. Remove the pasta from the water with tongs or drain the pasta, reserving a cup or so of the pasta water in the pot. Return the drained pasta to your pot and add your sauce to combine for serving.

If you want to try to cook pasta at your tailgate site, cook the pasta longer than your recipe predicts solely due to less heat. If you cook pasta in water less than boiling, stir frequently to keep the pasta from sticking to the bottom of the pan. A pasta pot with a built-in mesh container for draining also helps facilitate the process versus trying to drain your pasta in a colander. Reserve a cup or two of pasta water once the pasta has been cooked, depending on the magnitude of pasta you are preparing. Add the pasta water to the drained pasta. This will help the pasta stay moist and reduce the chance of stickiness.

Experiment with some of the recipes included in this book by changing the ingredients. Examples:
• Use the Shashlyk or Apple, Onion, and Sausage
  game plan but grill pieces of chicken with zucchini

and onions in a teriyaki sauce.

• Modify the game plan for Chili and substitute your favorite chili recipe.

• Make San Francisco's infamous "Joe's Special" using the Frittata game plan with eggs, cheese, spinach and ground beef.

• Alter the Paella recipe with your favorite stew concoction.

Most important in converting your recipe into a tailgate event is to think through and organize all the ingredients you will need at least a day before the event. We try to prepack as much as possible the night before so it's not so hectic getting ready the next morning.

RECIPES

PANCAKES AND SAUSAGE

This technique may be used for any pancake recipe. Remember to mix all of the dry ingredients in a heavy-duty, freezer-style, plastic bag to take to the tailgate with you. Then mix the wet ingredients with the dry portion in the bag once you are at your tailgate location. Ask one of your tailgate participants to bring links or a large ring of sausage. The sausage is easily cooked on a gas grill. We accompany the pancakes and sausage with a side of fresh fruit, Bloody Mary's, or Mimosas in warm weather. In colder weather, we enjoy lots of hot coffee and hot chocolate spiked with Bailey's, schnapps, and whipped cream. Each of the following recipes will produce fourteen pancakes.

BLUEBERRY PANCAKES

Ingredients

1 3/4 cups all-purpose flour
2 tablespoons sugar
1 teaspoon salt
1 teaspoon baking soda
2 teaspoons baking powder
2 cups buttermilk or sour milk
2 eggs, lightly beaten, or 1/2 cup egg substitute
3 tablespoons vegetable oil
1 cup fresh or frozen blueberries, drained
Maple syrup
Soft spreadable butter or margarine
Cooking oil spray

Utensils and Equipment

Cookplate or stove (propane)
Large skillet or griddle
Spatula
Heavy-duty aluminum foil
Gallon-size heavy-duty plastic bag
1 medium to large mixing bowl
1 small to medium mixing bowl
Tablespoon measuring spoon
Medium-sized whisk
1/4 cup measuring cup

CORN KERNEL PANCAKES

Ingredients

1 1/4 cups cornmeal
1/4 cup all-purpose flour
1/2 teaspoon salt
1/2 teaspoon freshly ground pepper
1/2 teaspoon baking soda
2 cups buttermilk
2 eggs, lightly beaten, or 1/2 cup egg substitute
3 tablespoons vegetable oil
1/2 cup frozen corn kernels, thawed
Maple syrup
Soft spreadable butter or margarine
Cooking oil spray

Utensils and Equipment

Cookplate or stove (propane)
Large skillet or griddle
Spatula
Heavy-duty aluminum foil
Gallon-size heavy-duty plastic bag
1 medium to large mixing bowl
1 small to medium mixing bowl
Tablespoon measuring spoon
Medium-sized whisk
1/4 cup measuring cup

Game Plan

The night before the tailgate, sift the dry ingredients into a plastic bag. Seal and put in your picnic basket. Premeasure the corn or blueberries, depending on which recipe you are using, in a plastic bag. The corn may be stored in the refrigerator or freezer overnight; either way the corn will be thawed by the time you reach your tailgate party. However, keep the blueberries in the freezer. They will get mushy if they thaw too much. I also try to purchase the buttermilk and egg substitute in the size that is needed for the recipe. If you use the exact recipe described above, a pint of buttermilk and the two egg individual serving size of egg substitute works well. You will then only need to a pack one quarter-cup measuring cup and a tablespoon for the oil. Consolidate the remaining ingredients in your refrigerator for easy retrieval for quick packing the morning of the tailgate. Pack the cookstove, skillet, spatula, measuring spoon, cup, and oil in the picnic basket or car.

The morning of the tailgate party, pack the picnic basket with the premeasured dry ingredients, if you have not already done so, corn or blueberries, and remaining ingredients, and head for your tailgate location.

Once you reach your tailgate location, unpack and provide your guests with the liquid refreshment planned for the day. When you are ready to eat, light the propane cookplate or cookstove and another heat source, such as the grill, if you are having sausage. Be careful not to cook the fare much before the guests are ready to eat. This meal is better eaten as the cakes and sausage are finished cooking and served right out of the pan. However, if you need to keep pancakes and sausage warm, wrap the cakes and sausage in separate packages of heavy-duty aluminum foil and place on the edge of the grill.

Place your skillet on the propane plate or cookstove and warm up to medium-high heat. Your skillet is hot enough when a drop of water skitters across your cooking surface. While the skillet is heating up, mix your wet ingredients with the dry ingredients by placing the plastic bag of dry ingredients in your medium- to large-sized mixing bowl. Do not empty the ingredients into the bowl; simply place the bag with the dry ingredients into the bowl. In the small- to medium-sized bowl, beat eggs, mix in buttermilk and oil, and combine the wet ingredients without the corn or blueberries using your whisk. Pour the wet ingredients into the bag with the dry ingredients. Add the corn if making the Corn Kernel Pancakes. Seal the bag and massage it to mix all of the ingredients. If you are making the Blueberry Pancakes, massage the plastic bag to mix thoroughly all ingredients except the blueberries. You will add the blueberries as you drop the batter onto the skillet instead of premixing.

When your skillet is hot, spray the surface with cooking oil spray if necessary. Then scoop up a quarter cup of batter from the plastic bag and pour onto the skillet. Cook two to three, or four if your skillet is large enough, at the same time. If you are making blueberry pancakes, pour the batter on the skillet and then sprinkle with blueberries. Your pancake will be ready to flip when bubbles form and the edges are cooked. Flip and brown the other side. Ask your participants to pick up a plate and receive, directly from the skillet, two or more pancakes and sausage off of the grill. Again, if you need to keep the cakes warm, wrap in heavy-duty aluminum foil and place on the edge of the grill. Continue until the pancake batter is depleted.

SKILLET FRITTATA

This recipe does not require any early preparation except for the gathering of ingredients and some chopping of onions, mushrooms, and vegetables. The rest is cooked at your tailgate. The success of this dish, however, is in the amount of control you have over the heat source or cookplate/stove. You may want to try this at home to learn how quickly the eggs cook on a low heat as a practice run in preparation for how to control the cookplate or stove. This recipe will generously feed six. An appetizer that works well with this entree is bagels with assorted toppings of cream cheese and caviar, chopped onion, and tomatoes, for starters, and a fruit salad as a side dish.

Ingredients

1 lb spicy bulk Italian sausage
1 dozen eggs (real eggs work better than egg substitute)
1 medium to large sweet onion, chopped
1 lb button or shiitake mushrooms, sliced
1 large red or yellow sweet bell pepper, chopped
2 cups chopped or sliced vegetables: zucchini, summer
   squash, fresh spinach, swiss chard or escarole lettuce
   (frozen spinach may be used once thawed and
   squeezed)
1 large clove garlic
Cooking oil spray

Utensils and Equipment

Propane cookplate or cookstove
Large cast iron or heavy-duty skillet with cover or
  heavy-duty aluminum foil
Spatula
Large serving spoon

Game Plan

The night before the tailgate, chop and slice the onion, mushrooms, pepper, and vegetables. Place the chopped or sliced ingredients in plastic bags; feel free to put the onions and peppers in the same bag, but keep the mushrooms and other vegetables in separate bags. Collect the rest of your ingredients in your refrigerator so that you may easily place them in your cooler the next morning. Pack your cookplate, skillet, and spatula in the car if you are packing the night before; otherwise, have them ready to be packed in the morning.

The next morning, finish packing your refrigerated items in your cooler for loading into the car.

Once you reach your tailgate destination, set out your appetizers and equip everyone with their favorite drink, then proceed with cooking your frittata. Turn on or light your cookplate or cookstove and set at medium-high heat. Spray your skillet with cooking oil and place on the cookplate to heat up. Once your skillet is somewhat hot (medium to medium-high heat) place the chopped onion and pepper in the skillet and sauté by stirring frequently until the onion is tender but not translucent. Add the mushrooms and continue to sauté until the onion is translucent and the mushrooms start to soften.

Add the Italian sausage, breaking it up until it is mixed with the previous ingredients and browned. Add your chopped or sliced vegetables and continue to sauté until the vegetables are wilted or crisp tender in the case of the squash. Stir the mixture thoroughly and then add the eggs. Break each egg quickly into the mixture and stir the whole concoction together as if you were scrambling the eggs while folding them into the meat and vegetable mixture. Lower the heat on the cookstove to low to medium-low and cover your skillet with your cover or heavy-duty aluminum foil as tightly as possible. After 5 minutes, grab your spatula and lift the lid on the pan. Carefully run the spatula around the edge of the pan across the bottom, picking up the egg mixture so that the uncooked eggs flow to the underside of the frittata. Cover again and check periodically for burning if you cannot control the heat. If the cookplate is too hot to slowly bake the frittata, use your spatula to gently fold the mixture in the pan from time to time to cook through.

Take this time to replenish your drink and announce that the frittata will be ready in 20 minutes. Uncover the skillet after 15 minutes and check to see if all of the egg is cooked through. If it is not, using your spatula, scoop up the mixture and fold it over so that you have shifted the undercooked portion to the bottom of the pan. Cover and cook for an additional 5 to 10 minutes, depending on how

fast the frittata is cooking. Uncover and dish out right
from the skillet. Cover, if all is not consumed during the
first round, for seconds.

SAKE MARINATED GRILLED SHRIMP

This recipe may be used for either a main entree or a great warm appetizer. The marinade also works on chicken wings for a great grilled appetizer. If you are planning to have the shrimp as an entree, plan on four to six jumbo shrimp for each person at your tailgate. For an appetizer, plan on two to three jumbo shrimp. I purchase frozen raw jumbo shrimp, cleaned and deveined, in the shell. Fresh shrimp also works well, but you will have to clean and devein. Leave the shell on. Make sure you have plenty of "Wet Ones" for yourself during the skewering of the shrimp before cooking and for your guests, since they will peel and eat.

Ingredients

36 to 40 raw jumbo shrimp for entree, thawed if frozen
(12 to 20 for appetizer)
3/4 cup chopped, peeled, fresh ginger
6 to 8 cloves garlic, squeezed
1/4 cup sugar
2 cups sake
3/4 cup soy sauce
Freshly ground black pepper

Utensils and Equipment

Kettle grill, gas or charcoal
Grilling tongs
Grilling brush
11 x 17 inch aluminum foil pan
Heavy-duty aluminum foil
1 jumbo-size freezer plastic bag
10 ten-inch bamboo skewers
Premoistened towels such as Wet Ones

Game Plan

Two days before your tailgate, purchase and thaw your frozen shrimp, if frozen, overnight in the refrigerator.

The night before your tailgate, mix your ginger, garlic, sugar, sake, soy sauce, and a generous grating of black pepper in a blender or food processor. Place cleaned, deveined shrimp in a jumbo-size plastic bag. Add the marinade. Refrigerate overnight. Gather the rest of your equipment for loading in your tailgate vehicle the next morning.

The morning of your tailgate, pack the picnic basket and cooler with all of the ingredients and supplies.

When you reach your tailgate destination, set out the appetizers, provide everyone their favorite drink, and light your grill using the direct method. While the grill is heating up to medium-hot, place the bamboo skewers and enough wine or water to cover them in the 11 x 17 aluminum foil pan and soak for at least 15 minutes. Once the skewers have had time to soak, remove them from the pan and toss out all of the liquid. Place the skewers back in the pan to one side for your access while you skewer the shrimp. Thread the shrimp belly to back, so that they face in the same direction and lay flat, directly out of the plastic bag. Thread five to six shrimp per skewer. Place in the aluminum pan. Use the premoistened towels or Wet Ones to clean yourself up after the skewering process.

When the grill is ready, or medium-hot, place the shrimp on the grill. Cover your grill with the lid and leave for 5 minutes. While the shrimp are cooking, line the aluminum pan with clean heavy-duty aluminum foil to provide a place for your cooked shrimp for serving. Turn the skewered shrimp over and cover for another 3 to 5 minutes. Remove the shrimp from the grill when they are opaque and pink. Have your guests take a skewer to start and cover the aluminum pan with foil to keep warm, if necessary.

MIXED SAUSAGES IN BEER

My father-in-law says that we have not had a successful tailgate season unless we have one party serving grilled sausages. We usually mix up the sausages by using Bratwurst, Polish, and both hot and sweet Italian types. The assorted mustards include a sweet honey mustard, a spicy brown mustard, and a sharp Dijon. This recipe allows you to start the entree anytime since the sausages stay moist in the beer until you finish them off over the coals. Make sure you serve the sausages with Mother-in-Law's Beans. This recipe will generously feed six.

Ingredients

8 to 12 fresh sausages
8 to 12 hot dog buns, freshly baked if available
6 to 8 cans of beer
Condiments: assorted mustards and ketchup
Garnishes: chopped onion, peppers, and shredded
   cheese
Cooking oil spray

Utensils and Equipment

Kettle grill, gas or charcoal
Grilling tongs
Two 12-inch square deep aluminum foil pans
Heavy-duty aluminum foil

Game Plan

The night before your tailgate, purchase your sausages, hot dog buns, beer, condiments, and garnishes. I have located a bakery capable of baking fresh hot dog buns if I place an order with them earlier in the week. Some grocery stores with bakeries also provide this service. I also call my butcher early in the week and order the assorted sausages, freshly stuffed rather than buying commercially prepared. Commercially manufactured sausages will work if you do not have access to fresh sausages.

That same night, clean and chop the onions and peppers. Place in separate plastic bags, tightly sealed, for storage in the refrigerator overnight. Gather all of the condiments and beer in one spot for quick packing the morning of the tailgate party.

The morning of your tailgate, pack the picnic basket and cooler with all of the ingredients and supplies.

Once you reach your tailgate location, the guests armed with appetizers and their favorite beverage, start the grill using the direct method. When the grill reaches medium-hot heat, spray your grill rack with cooking oil spray and place on the grill. Set one of the aluminum foil pans on the grill. Fill the aluminum pan halfway in volume with the beer. Place half of the assorted sausages into the beer and heat up on the grill. When your guests are ready for the entree, place a beer soaked sausage on the grill using your tongs and grill until browned on all sides, about 5 minutes, turning frequently. Tongs are important, as op-

posed to a grilling fork; puncturing the sausages with a
fork while cooking will release the juices, resulting in a
dry cooked sausage. Ask you guests to obtain a bun for
their sausage and have them augment it with the condiments and garnishes.

LAMB BURGERS

...ili entree included in this book, this spicy ...ernative to the traditional hamburger. Try ...arm weather tailgate party with whole ...d the assortment of "deluxe" accompani- ...d below. You will note that the ground beef content in this recipe may range from a half to a full pound, depending on your taste for lamb. I have made the patties entirely with lamb, which turn out marvelous as well. French bread rolls or lightly toasted or grilled slices of Italian, Greek, or peasant bread may be substituted for the whole wheat rolls.

Ingredients

1 lb ground lamb
1/2 to 1 lb lean ground beef, preferably sirloin or round
1/4 cup grated onion
1 tablespoon squeezed or minced garlic
1 tablespoon extra virgin olive oil
2 tablespoons chopped fresh parsley
1 teaspoon crushed dried oregano
1 teaspoon cinnamon
1 teaspoon ground cumin
1/2 teaspoon freshly ground pepper
8 whole wheat hamburger buns or slices of Italian, Greek
   or peasant bread (bring extra olive oil if using bread
   instead of buns)
Cooking oil spray

Garnishes

2 sweet green peppers, seeded and thinly sliced
3 ripe plum tomatoes, thinly sliced
1 red onion, halved and slivered
1 cup crumbled gorgonzola or blue cheese
Mayonnaise

Utensils and Equipment

Grill, gas or charcoal
8-inch aluminum foil pan
Grilling spatula
One-gallon food storage bag
4 sandwich or quart-size food storage bags

Game Plan

The night before your tailgate party, combine in a large bowl all of the ingredients except the buns and garnishes. Work together with your hands to combine. Do not over mix. Form meat into eight patties, about 1 inch thick and 4 inches across. Place into a plastic bag and store in the refrigerator until the morning of your tailgate party. If you are preparing the day you plan to grill, prepare a couple hours ahead to allow the spices time to mingle. Remember to bring to room temperature before you place the patties on the grill. Prepare the garnishes by cleaning, slicing, and packing them into separate small plastic bags. Gather the rest of your ingredients together in your re-frigerator for easy packing the next morning.

The morning of the tailgate, pack the garnishes, buns, and patties in your cooler.

Once you have arrived at your tailgate location, furnish all of your guests with their favorite beverage and appetizers and start the grill using the direct method. While the grill is heating up, unpack the garnishes and place on your serving table. We usually place the garnishes on a plate for easy access. Cover with plastic wrap if it is a warm day and you need to keep the critters off while you are grilling the main fare.

Once the grill is hot, spray the grill rack with cooking oil spray and place the rack on the grill. Wait 5 minutes before placing the patties on the grill to ensure that the rack is hot. Grill the lamb patties about 8 minutes on the first side and 5 minutes after turning for a rare burger. If you are using slices of bread instead of buns, brush the slices of bread with olive oil and grill on the edges of your grilling surface along with the burgers. Since this dish cooks quickly, announce to your fellow tailgaters that the burgers are ready and would they please grab a plate and queue up for serving. Serve hot off of the grill in the bun or slices of bread and garnish.

SAUSAGE, APPLE AND ONION
SHISH KEBAB

Here is a simple recipe that turns out fabulous. This is a great "last minute" entree since you probably have all of the ingredients readily at hand. We enjoy using both hot and sweet sausages to give the shish kebab a bit of zing. This recipe will generously feed six.

Ingredients

3 lbs Italian sausages, hot or sweet
6 large Macintosh or Granny Smith apples
6 large Vidalia or sweet onions
1 large lemon, squeezed
1/2 cup white wine
8 oz jar apple jelly

Utensils and Equipment

Kettle grill, gas or charcoal
Small mixing bowl
Grilling brush
Tongs
8 long metal or bamboo skewers
Medium whisk or wooden spoon
11 x 17 inch aluminum foil pan
Heavy-duty aluminum foil
3 large plastic bags, zipper or seal type

Game Plan

The night before your tailgate, clean and cut the cored apples and onions into quarters. Place in separate plastic bags. Tightly seal the bag of onions. Pour freshly squeezed lemon juice into the bag of cut apples to retard discoloring while in storage. Seal the bag tightly. Massage the apples in the bag to coat evenly, then refrigerate the bags of apples and onions. Cut the sausages into 2-inch chunks and place in a plastic bag for storage in the refrigerator overnight.

The morning of your tailgate party, load the bags of onions, apples, and sausages, the apple jelly, and the wine into your picnic basket or cooler. Don't forget the utensils, especially the skewers!

When you arrive at your tailgate location and you are set up with appetizers and drinks, prepare the apple jelly and wine baste. Spoon the apple jelly into your small mixing bowl. Whisk the white wine thoroughly into the jelly. The baste should be thick like a slippery honey. Don't be concerned about any lumps that are still in the baste – it will not matter when you paint it onto the shish kebabs.

Next, set up the grill in the direct method and light. Once the grill is lit, get out your skewers and bags of apples, onions, and sausages. Thread the items alternatively on the skewers and place in the 11 x 17 inch aluminum foil pan. Baste the skewers while in the pan. Cover with heavy-duty aluminum foil or plastic wrap until the grill is a medium-hot. When the grill has reached the desired heat,

place the skewers on the grill and baste again, if necessary, dabbing out the baste drippings from the aluminum
pan. Grill a total of 15 to 20 minutes, turning and basting
every 5 minutes. Line your aluminum pan with fresh
heavy-duty aluminum foil. Remove the skewers from the
grill when the apples are hot but not mushy. Push the
apples, onions, and sausages off the skewers into the aluminum pan and ask your tailgaters to help themselves.
Cover the remaining kebabs in the aluminum pan with
heavy-duty foil to help them stay warm until your guests
are ready for seconds.

BARBECUED RIBS AND/OR CHICKEN

Get ready for plenty of passersby to career near your grill for a whiff of this entree. We have even had tailgaters ask if they could purchase some of our fare. Usually we are not able to accommodate their request because our tailgate party devours every bit we grill. Two different methods of grilling this fare are included. The first method, using heavy-duty aluminum foil, is a method to use if you do not want to tend to the grill every 5 minutes or so. The second method, using an indirect grilling process, demands more of your time, although some prefer the latter method for its flavor. This recipe will generously feed six.

Ingredients

1 frying chicken, cut into serving-size pieces, or 4
    breasts and 4 legs and thighs
6 to 8 country-style ribs
Your favorite smoky and spicy barbecue sauce
Cooking oil spray

Utensils and Equipment

Kettle grill, gas or charcoal
Grilling fork
Grilling brush
Grilling tongs

11 x 17 inch aluminum foil pan
Small bowl
Heavy-duty aluminum foil

Game Plan

Heavy-Duty Aluminum Foil Method

The night before your tailgate, wash and pat dry all of your chicken and/or ribs. Set aside. Tear off a generous rectangle of heavy-duty aluminum foil. Lay the foil down on your counter shiny side up. Spray the entire interior of the rectangle generously with cooking oil spray; edges do not need to be sprayed. Then drizzle barbecue sauce on the foil and spread to cover a middle section of the foil that consists of the area your meat will cover.

Place your meat, either your chicken or your ribs, on top of the sauced area. Do not place the chicken and ribs to-gether in the same foil packet. Depending on the type of chicken pieces you have, you may want to place the larger denser parts, like the breasts, in a separate packet from the wings and legs, since the latter cook faster. Separate packets allow you to place the smaller pieces on the edge of a hot fire for slower cooking.

Place your chicken skin side up or, in the case of the ribs, place the ribs standing up side by side or, in other words, balanced upright on their flattest cut narrow edge. Once you have the meat positioned on the foil, drizzle more sauce on top of your meat and spread. Now pull the short ends of your rectangle up to form a tent over the meat. With the two short edges together, fold tightly down to the meat, folding the foil over and over in a fashion similar to folding a paper lunch bag. Once the short ends are folded, repeat the fold at the other two ends so that you end up with a sealed packet. Now repeat this process using another rectangle sheet of foil the same size as your first sheet, except this time you will place the foil on your counter shiny side down. Place your sealed packet in the foil, seamed or folded side down similar to folding a paper bag, and wrap again so that your packets have two layers of foil. Make sure your seals are tight and you do not have any holes in the packet for the sauce to escape. If you have a problem with the sauce seeping out through a hole or seam, wrap the package again with foil.

When you complete the wrapping process for all of the chicken and ribs you plan to grill, place them in your refrigerator overnight or, if you plan to grill the same day, refrigerate until 1 hour before you grill. You will need to set the packets out to bring the meat to room temperature before grilling.

One last task the night before: make sure you bring more barbecue sauce for basting while you are grilling. Two additional cups of sauce should be adequate for the amount of meat listed above. Be sure to pack your grilling tongs, fork, and brush!

The morning of your tailgate party, load your foil packets into your car. No need to keep the chicken or ribs on ice since they will need to warm up a bit before grilling.

A caveat to this rule of bringing your meat to room temperature: when it is a warm day and you do not plan to grill your fare for two or more hours after you remove the packets from the refrigerator, you will need to keep your meat chilled.

When you reach your tailgate destination, set out the appetizers, supply everyone with their favorite drink, and light your grill using the direct method. Spray your grill rack with cooking oil spray and place it on the grill after you spread your hot coals. When the grill is ready, or medium-hot, place the packets on the grill, seam or fold side down, cover your grill with the lid, and leave for 15 minutes. Turn the packet over and leave for another 15 minutes.

After 30 to 35 minutes of cooking in the foil packets, it is time to unwrap your barbecued entree. Pull the packets to the edge of your grill and, using your grilling fork, puncture one of the packets and tear the foil back. The foil will be filled with lots of juice so be careful while you pull the meat out to place on the grill. Using tongs, place the chicken skin side up and lay the ribs on their widest side. Pour the sauce from the packet over the meat on the grill and cover with the lid for 5 to 8 minutes, depending how hot the fire is. Keep a watch to make sure your food does not burn. When you lift the cover, dab on more barbecue sauce and turn the chicken and ribs over to brown. Dab more sauce on the side that is now up and cover the grill for another 5 to 8 minutes. You may need to move your meat around on the grill if some pieces are cooking faster than others. Your chicken and ribs should be done by now, but if they need a bit more time, dab on more sauce and keep turning. Announce to all that dinner is served, remove the grilled entree to the 11 x 17 inch aluminum foil pan, and place on your serving table.

Indirect Grilling Process

The night before your tailgate, wash and pat dry all of your chicken and/or ribs. Place chicken in a separate plastic bag from the ribs. Pack the rest of your ingredients and utensils, remembering to bring at least 3 cups of your favorite barbecue sauce.

The morning of your tailgate party, load your ingredients and equipment into your car. If you plan to grill the chicken and ribs less than one hour after you remove them from the refrigerator, there is no need to keep the chicken or ribs on ice since they will need to warm up a bit before grilling. A caveat to this rule is that when it is a warm day or you do not plan to grill your fare for more than one hour after you remove the chicken and ribs from the refrigerator, you will need to keep your meat chilled.

When you reach your tailgate destination, set out the appetizers, supply everyone with their favorite drink, and set up your grill in a modified indirect method. The modified indirect method involves placing your charcoal to one side of your grill versus the split indirect method. With this approach, split your grill in half and pile your charcoal up to one side of your imaginary diagonal split line. Light your charcoal and spread it, when hot, within your designated half of the grill. Spray your grill rack with cooking oil spray and place on the grill after you spread your hot coals. Get out the chicken and ribs and place them in the aluminum pan, skin side up in the case of the chicken. Spray the fare with cooking oil spray to prevent it from sticking to the grill. Pour your barbecue sauce into a small bowl and set on the table near your barbecue along with your grilling utensils. Cover with heavy-duty aluminum foil to keep the critters out.

If your entree is chilled, cover the pan with heavy-duty aluminum foil and let it sit to bring it to room temperature. Warming the meat to room temperature is important with this method. If your meat is cold when you put it on the grill, you run the risk of cooking the outside without fully cooking the inside, especially with the chicken.

When the grill is ready or medium-hot, place the chicken and ribs on the grill, oil-sprayed side down first. Cover your grill with the lid and leave for 5 to 8 minutes, depending on how hot your fire is. Check frequently to prevent burning. Once your fare is browned on the initial side, turn it over with your tongs, dab on barbecue sauce and cover for another 5 to 8 minutes. Continue to turn and coat with barbecue sauce every 5 to 8 minutes, moving the pieces to the side of the grill without direct heat when the sauce starts to burn. Your entree should be fully cooked after a total grilling time of 30 to 35 minutes. A method of checking doneness is to poke a sharp knife or fork into the thickest piece of chicken. If the juices run clear, the chicken is cooked. Line your aluminum foil pan with fresh heavy-duty aluminum foil. Announce to all that dinner is served, remove the grilled entree to the freshly

lined aluminum foil pan, and place it on your serving table.
Cover the pan with heavy-duty aluminum foil to keep the
food warm.

PAELLA

This recipe for Paella is the same as any cook's recipe, except that it has been adapted for a tailgate event. This adaptation accomplishes two objectives: first, to minimize the need to wash dishes and, second, to have time to socialize while cooking the meal. This recipe serves twelve hungry folks.

Ingredients

1 lb or 4 six-inch chorizo sausages
3 lbs skinned and boned chicken breasts
2 lobster tails
1 lb medium shrimp
1/2 lb small to medium scallops
12 cherrystone clams, washed
12 mussels, washed and debearded
1 cup extra virgin olive oil
10 oz frozen peas
2 large sweet yellow peppers, chopped
2 large Spanish or Vidalia onions, chopped
5 cloves garlic, squeezed or minced
2 cups uncooked rice
8 cups chicken stock
4 large tomatoes, peeled, seeded, and chopped
1/2 teaspoon powdered saffron
Salt and freshly ground pepper

Utensils and Equipment

Grill, gas or charcoal
Cookplate (propane)
12 bamboo skewers
Large stock pot or kettle
Large spoon (grill utensil type)
Wooden cutting board
Sharp butcher knife
11 x 17 aluminum foil pan
Garlic press or squeezer
Can opener if using canned stock
Grilling tongs
Grilling brush
Heavy-duty aluminum foil
Premoistened napkins or towelettes
1/4 cup measuring cup

Game Plan

The day or two before your tailgate party, freeze the fresh seafood items if you purchased them earlier than the day before the tailgate party. Any fresh seafood you purchase for your tailgate party should be kept well chilled until you are ready to cook. Since seafood is dangerous if left at room temperature too long, I find that working with partially frozen items ensures freshness and eliminates the chance of spoilage. Therefore, I place fresh items in the freezer for a day and, the night before the tailgate, move them to the refrigerator.

The night before the tailgate, place all frozen items, except the peas, in the refrigerator to start thawing. Assemble all of the ingredients so they can be loaded quickly the next morning without much worry.

In separate plastic bags:
  • Cut the chicken breasts into 2-inch cubes
  • Chop the onion and yellow pepper
  • Peel, seed, and chop the tomatoes
  • Measure out the rice

Clean the mussels and clams. Devein the shrimp in the shell and rinse the scallops if they have not already been cleaned. This step may be accomplished the day you purchase the seafood, if fresh. Then freeze after cleaning. I usually buy frozen mussels and clams that have already been cleaned and frozen shrimp that has been deveined in the shell, so all I have to do is thaw. Place the cleaned seafood in two plastic bags, separating the mussels and clams from the shrimp. Freeze or refrigerate, depending on the amount of time the seafood will sit in a cooler.

Pack all items (food and utensils) that do not need to be refrigerated in your picnic basket or whatever container you plan to use. Get out your cooler and have it ready to load the refrigerated items. If you do not have ice at home to fill your cooler in the morning, buy ice on the way to the game and dump a bag over the items that need to be chilled. Gather all of the refrigerated items together in one spot in your refrigerator to help you remember everything the next morning.

The morning of your tailgate, pack your cooler with the refrigerated items and the frozen peas with lots of ice. Some of the items may still be frozen, but by the time you add them to your pot or place them on the grill, they will be thawed. If you are making this at home with the refrigerator accessible, fresh seafood works well without freezing.

Once you arrive at your tailgate location, set up tables, unload the cooler and picnic basket, put the drinks and appetizers out, and place the cookplate at the end of one of the picnic tables with the grill nearby. Situate the cutting board to either side of the hot plate. Arrange all of your ingredients near your cookplate and grill for easy access. Get out your cooking utensils and soak the bamboo skewers in water in the aluminum pan. Greet your invited guests and provide them with a drink while the skewers soak.

Since this is a complicated recipe, along with the fact that grilling has been determined to be a skill of the male side of the human species, we usually have fellow tailgaters help with the Paella. If you do not have one designee assigned to manage the grill, feel free to invite the guys to do the grilling.

Start the grill using the direct method. Arm the folks who want to help with skewers. Skewer the scallops first, shrimp second, and the chicken last and lay the skewered items in the emptied aluminum pan you used to soak the bamboo skewers. Add to the pan the chorizo sausage and the lobster tails. Brush all the items in the pan lightly with olive oil. Cover with heavy-duty aluminum foil until the fire in the grill is ready. Provide premoistened napkins or towelettes to your helpers for cleanup.

While the grill is heating and the fare is being skewered, turn on your cookplate to a moderately high heat. Coat the bottom of your stock pot with 1/4 cup of olive oil and let it heat for a couple of minutes. Then add to your pot the chopped yellow pepper, onion, and garlic and sauté, stirring frequently with your large spoon, until the onion is translucent. Add to this mixture the rice and sauté for 5 minutes. Add 6 cups of chicken stock, tomatoes, saffron, salt, and pepper. Bring to a boil, then reduce the heat just enough to keep a simmer going with the top on.

Once the grill reaches a moderate temperature, place the grill rack on the grill and allow some time for it to heat up. When the grill rack is hot, roast the items listed below in the following order, or the longest to the least cooking time:

1. Chorizo sausages: 15 to 20 minutes
2. Whole lobsters: 15 minutes
3. Chicken breasts: 10 minutes or until opaque
4. Shrimp: 8 minutes or until just pink
5. Scallops: 5 minutes

Using tongs, grill the sausages first. After the sausages have cooked for 10 minutes start the lobsters. Remove the sausages after the next 10 minutes have passed and start the chicken. When you remove the chicken, grill the shrimp and scallops. Because the mixture cooks as it is added to the pot, all of the grilled fare does not have to be fully cooked (although I do fully cook the sausage), so don't worry if the chicken is a bit pink. Let the lobster cool slightly before cutting it up so you can handle it with your hands. It will cook more as it cools so be careful not to overcook.

As the grilled items are removed from the grill, place them on the cutting board next to your stock pot. Slice the sausages into 1 inch chunks and cut the lobster into chunks before you add it to your stock pot. Otherwise, add the grilled items to the pot as they are removed from the grill and stir each time you add an item. Remember to remove the bamboo skewers, where you have used them, before adding the meat and shellfish to your pot. The rice should be done but not mushy at this point. If the rice still has a bite to it, add 1 to 2 more cups of chicken stock. Stir your concoction, cover, and lower the heat to keep it from burning. Check after 10 to 15 minutes.

When the rice is cooked, add the peas, shrimp, scallops, mussels, and clams as your last step. Stir, cover, and announce to all that dinner is ready. By the time the salad is uncovered, the bread is sliced, and the flavored butters are unwrapped, you can uncover the pot and stir the Paella for the last time before serving. The mussels and clam shells should open at this point. Caution your guests to discard any shells that do not open. Invite them to help themselves and make sure they are welcome for seconds.

TERIYAKI SALMON

The real key to this recipe is to find especially fresh salmon. I usually order my fish from the meat market where I do most of my business, and Jerry, the butcher, makes sure I have fresh fish. If I have to purchase some-place else, the fishmonger puts up with me smelling what he is trying to sell or I buy frozen as a last resort. If the fish smells the least bit fishy, don't buy it. Fresh salmon does not have a strong fishy smell; it should smell more like salt water or the ocean. This recipe will serve six.

Ingredients

Six 1/2 lb salmon fillets
1/2 cup soy sauce
1/2 cup rice vinegar
1/2 cup Asian-style sesame oil
1/2 cup extra virgin olive oil
2 tablespoons hot chili oil (Asian variety)
4 cloves garlic, minced or pressed
Freshly ground pepper
Cooking oil spray

Utensils and Equipment

Grill, gas or charcoal
Grilling tongs
1 square aluminum foil pan
1 jumbo-size plastic freezer bag
Heavy-duty aluminum foil

Game Plan

The night before your tailgate party, purchase your fish. Thoroughly rinse the fish in cold water and place it on paper towels to drain while you prepare the marinade. In a bowl large enough to blend a little over 2 cups of marinade, whisk together soy sauce, rice vinegar, sesame oil, and olive oil. Add hot chili oil, garlic, and pepper and blend well.

Pat the fish dry if it has not drained sufficiently. The fish should not be wet when you add it to the marinade. Depending on the number of fillets you intend to grill, select a gallon or jumbo-size freezer-style plastic bag. Lay the fish in the bag, double-layered if necessary, and pour the marinade in the bag. Seal the bag and move the fillets around so that all are covered with the marinade. Place the bag overnight in the refrigerator. Flip the bag occasionally to ensure that all of the fillets are covered with marinade.

The morning of the tailgate party, transfer the fish in the marinade from the refrigerator to a cooler for your trip to the tailgate. If it takes you less than 30 minutes to reach your tailgate location and you plan to start your grill right after you set up your equipment, packing the fish in a cooler is not necessary. As mentioned earlier, your food should be at room temperature before it is placed on the grill to ensure that each item cooks evenly. Therefore, let the fish reach 65 to 70 degrees by removing it from the cooler or refrigerator 1 hour before grilling.

When you reach your tailgate destination, set out all of the appetizers, supply everyone with their favorite drink, and light your grill using the direct method. Remove the fish from the marinade and place it in the aluminum pan to drain a bit before you place the fillets on the grill. Spray your grill rack with cooking oil spray. When the grill reaches a medium-hot temperature, spread the coals and place the rack on the grill. Heat the rack 5 minutes before grilling the fish. Place fillets skin side down on the heated oiled grill rack. Grill about 10 to 15 minutes per inch with the skin side down, depending on how cooked you like your fish. Turn the fish and grill for 10 minutes longer at the most. Grill skin side down for the major portion of your cooking time. Chances are that the skin will stick to the grill when you flip the fish over, which is fine. Usually, once cooked, it will not stick to the rack when you turn it. A method for checking doneness of the fish is to insert a fork into the thickest portion of the fillet and carefully pull it apart so that you can see how opaque the fish is. We happen to like salmon a little on the rare side but if you like fish fully cooked the flesh should be opaque. Take care not to overcook, because your fish will dry out.

Announce to your tailgate partiers that the fish is ready and either remove it from the grill onto a serving plate or have the partygoers line up at the grill to be served. If you plan to use your aluminum pan as a serving pan, line it with fresh foil to minimize contamination between the raw and cooked fish. Cover the pan with heavy-duty aluminum foil to keep the fish warm. This same recipe may be used for meats, such as steak or lamb, if you add 1/2 cup or equal parts of full bodied red wine, like a cabernet or merlot.

GRILLED, ROLLED AND STUFFED TURKEY BREAST

This dish takes some preparation a day or two before your tailgate party. But once you get it on the grill, you will have a good hour of cooking time, so you may socialize with your guests. This recipe will generously feed six.

Ingredients

One 3 to 4 lb or two 2 lb turkey breasts, with skin, boned and flattened with a mallet
1 lb Italian sausage
1 large Granny Smith apple, peeled and finely chopped
1 large Spanish or Vidalia onion, finely chopped
Freshly ground pepper
2 cups extra virgin olive oil
2 large cloves garlic
Cooking oil spray

Utensils and Equipment

Kettle grill, gas or charcoal
Wooden cutting board
Heavy-duty aluminum foil
11 x 17 drip pan
Roast rack
Sharp carving knife

Grilling fork
Brush for garlic oil
Meat thermometer
Kitchen string or cord to tie up the turkey

Game Plan

One week before your event, peel and crush the garlic cloves and add to the olive oil. Set aside until the tailgate party. Also, if you do not want to bone and flatten your own turkey breast, call your butcher and ask him or her to procure and prepare the turkey for you. This is well worth the planning because it is a major job to flatten a large turkey breast with a mallet. The butcher will have the proper equipment to do this, which will make the job a lot easier for him and for you.

The night before your tailgate party, mix together thoroughly the sausage, apple, and onion. Spread out on your counter a piece of heavy-duty aluminum foil double the size of the turkey and spray it generously with cooking oil spray. Lay the turkey, without the skin, on the foil and spread the sausage mixture evenly across the turkey. Starting with the shorter end of the turkey, roll or fold over tightly and wrap the roll with the skin. (An extra set of hands usually comes in handy about now!!) Tie the roll with kitchen string about every 2 to 3 inches. Brush the skin with the garlic olive oil. Wrap the turkey roll in the heavy-duty aluminum foil by folding the edges tightly, first across the top and then the sides. Wrap again with another sheet of heavy-duty aluminum foil. Place the roll in the refrigerator until you load the car for your tailgate party. Also assemble the rest of your ingredients and equipment for packing the night before or the next morning. Do not forget the garlic olive oil.

The morning of the tailgate party, remove your foil-wrapped turkey breast from the refrigerator and pack in any container. Unless it is a hot day, there is no need to keep the turkey breast cold. The roll should be at room temperature before you put it on the grill. The time it takes you to get to your tailgate location should allow the roast to come to a warmer temperature so it will be ready when the grill is hot. Remember to pack the equipment arranged the night before.

When you reach your tailgate location, start the grill using the direct method. Then proceed with your setup by providing the appetizers and everyone's favorite drink. Once the charcoal is gray, put the turkey wrapped in foil on the roast rack in the 11 x 17 pan and place on top of the grill rack. Cover the grill and leave it for an hour without peeking. After an hour, remove the foil on the roast and, with the turkey still in the roast rack, brush on more garlicky olive oil and insert a meat thermometer set for 170 degrees into the thickest portion of the turkey breast. Put the lid back on the grill and leave it for 15 minutes. Baste the turkey again with the garlic olive oil. Cover the grill for another 15 minutes. Continue this process until the roast reaches 170 degrees. Remove it from the grill and wrap it in another sheet of heavy-duty aluminum foil. After it has rested for 10 minutes, cut into slices on the cutting board and invite your guests to dig in.

GRILLED, GLAZED CORNED BEEF

A fellow Michigan alumnus sent me this recipe with a note describing the established tradition among women of trading recipes. She commented that this behavior seems "rather cult-like." Since then, she has become one of my testers, bless her soul, and she has survived. Although this recipe requires some work, it will dazzle your guests with what can be done with a corned beef brisket. This recipe will serve six.

Ingredients

4 lbs corned beef brisket
12 black peppercorns
4 bay leaves
4 small, hot, whole red chilies
3 two to three inch cinnamon sticks, broken up
4 large cloves garlic, smashed
1 large onion, sliced
1/2 cup brown sugar, packed
1 teaspoon dry mustard
1/2 teaspoon ground cloves
1/2 teaspoon ground ginger
1/2 teaspoon celery salt
1/2 teaspoon cracked caraway seed
Cooking oil spray

Utensils and Equipment

Kettle grill, gas or charcoal
Wooden cutting board
11 x 17 drip pan
Roast rack
Sharp carving knife
Grilling fork
Jug of water
Heavy-duty aluminum foil

Game Plan

Two days before your tailgate party, place the corned beef in a large pot and cover with water. Add the bay leaves, chilies, cinnamon, peppercorns, garlic and onion. Bring to a boil, cover, lower heat, and simmer slowly for 4 to 4 1/2 hours or until the meat is tender. Drain in a colander and blot dry. While the roast is draining, prepare the rub by combining and smashing with a mortar and pestle the dry mustard, cloves, ginger, celery salt, and caraway seed. Mix into the brown sugar.

Tear off a sheet of heavy-duty aluminum foil about two and a half times the size of your roast and lay it shiny side up on your counter. Coat the center portion of the surface where the roast will come in contact with the foil with cooking oil spray. Place the corned beef in the center of the foil and rub the entire surface with the brown sugar and spice rub. Wrap the brisket in the foil by bringing the shorter edges together first and folding to seal and then folding the remaining edges to seal the brisket completely. Repeat this process, only this time place the foil shiny side down on the counter and do not spray with oil. Repeat the folding procedure so that your corned beef is double wrapped in foil. Place your wrapped brisket in the refrigerator until the morning of your tailgate party.

The night before your tailgate party, assemble or pack your equipment for the event the next day.

The morning of the tailgate party, remove your corned beef brisket from the refrigerator and pack in any container. Unless it is a hot day, there is no need to keep the brisket cold. The corned beef should be at room temperature before you put it on the grill. The time it takes you to get to your tailgate location should allow the roast to come to a warmer temperature so that it will be ready to be grilled. If your timing is longer than two hours before you put the brisket on the grill, keep your brisket chilled in a cooler until an hour before grilling.

When you reach your tailgate location, start the grill using the indirect method. Once the charcoal is gray and at medium heat, put the brisket wrapped in foil on the grill in the roast rack placed in the 11 x 17 pan on top of the grill rack. Pour three cups of water into the pan under the roast rack. Cover the grill and roast for 1 hour.

After an hour of roasting, unwrap the brisket and replace it in the roast rack. Pour any juice that accumulated in the foil into the drip pan. Insert a meat thermometer into the brisket and add more liquid, 1/2 to 1 cup, to the pan under the roast if necessary. Cover the grill for 20 minutes longer. Check the meat thermometer and remove the roast from the grill when the internal temperature reaches 140 degrees. Let the roast sit, covered with foil, for 15 minutes before carving. Announce to the tailgaters that the rest of the meal may be prepared and ask a volunteer to carve the brisket.

MOTHER-IN-LAW'S BEANS

My mother-in-law graciously volunteered this wonderful accompaniment. We always look forward to this unique dish. This bean side works well with other entrees provided in this cookbook, such as Mixed Sausages in Beer, Pork Roast with Orange Mustard Sauce, or Barbecued Ribs and/or Chicken. This recipe will generously serve ten.

Ingredients

15 oz canned dark kidney beans, drained
15 oz canned butter beans, drained
28 oz canned baked beans
1/4 lb bacon, cut up
1/2 large onion, chopped
1 tablespoon mustard
1/2 cup brown sugar
2 tablespoons vinegar
2 tablespoons molasses
1/2 cup ketchup
Dash of salt

Utensils and Equipment

2 quart casserole dish
Newspaper
Large serving spoon
Cookplate, if you plan to warm the beans up

Game Plan

The night before your tailgate party, fry the bacon and onion in a large glass casserole dish until the bacon is crisp and the onion cooked. If your casserole dish is not conducive to the high heat of a stove, fry the bacon and onion in a small frying pan and transfer them to the large casserole dish. Add all other ingredients. Bake at 300 degrees for 2 hours. Reduce heat to 150 degrees and bake for another hour. Remove and place in refrigerator overnight.

The morning of the tailgate party, microwave the bean mixture in the casserole dish on high for 10 minutes and then put it in a 350-degree oven to continue heating until you leave for the tailgate party. Wrap the casserole dish in lots of newspaper and then place it in a thermal container, like a cooler, or wrap it in a blanket and load it into your car to be transferred to your tailgate party.

When you reach your tailgate location, wait to unwrap your casserole until your entree is ready to be served. Unwrap the beans and place them on the table for serving. If you plan to heat your beans up on a cookplate, place the casserole or large pot of beans on the cookplate once you have arrived at the tailgate location. Turn on the cookplate to low and heat at least 1 1/2 to 2 hours, stirring occasionally to prevent the beans from burning. Serve the beans directly from the casserole dish or pot with your large serving spoon.

PORK ROAST WITH ORANGE MUSTARD SAUCE

Similar to the Grilled, Rolled and Stuffed Turkey Breast, this recipe takes a good 60 to 90 minutes to cook. If you do not have the time to fully cook a pork roast on the grill, then try pork chops 1 1/2 inches thick with this marinade for a faster pace. This entree will serve six hungry tailgaters.

Ingredients

4 lbs center cut pork roast
1/4 cup butter (unsalted preferred)
1 cup fresh orange juice
1/2 cup port or sweet red wine
1/4 cup firmly packed brown sugar
2 tablespoons balsamic or red wine vinegar
2 tablespoons soy sauce
1/2 cup Dijon-style mustard
4 to 5 cloves garlic, smashed and minced or pressed
1/2 cup minced fresh rosemary
   (or 1 tablespoon dried crushed rosemary)
1 tablespoon fresh gingerroot, minced or grated
Freshly ground pepper
2 1/3 cups water
1 tablespoon cornstarch
Cooking oil spray

Utensils and Equipment

Kettle grill, gas or charcoal
Grilling fork
Roast rack
11 x 17 inch drip pan
Heavy-duty aluminum foil
Cookplate
Saucepan (3 to 4 cup capacity)
Meat thermometer
Large spoon and ladle
2 jumbo-size plastic freezer bags

Game Plan

One to two nights before your tailgate party, marinate your pork roast in the orange mustard marinade. Begin preparing your marinade by melting the butter in a saucepan over low heat. Add the following ingredients and simmer until heated through, about five minutes: orange juice, wine, brown sugar, vinegar, soy sauce, mustard, rosemary, garlic, gingerroot, and pepper. Cool the marinade to lukewarm before combining with the meat. Place the pork roast in a plastic bag and pour the marinade over it. Seal and put this bag in another plastic bag and seal tightly. Refrigerate overnight or until the morning of your tailgate party. Flip the roast occasionally while in the refrigerator to ensure adequate coverage while marinating.

Premeasure the water by filling a container with at least 3 cups. Also pack your cornstarch in a small plastic bag. Pack these two items in the picnic basket for transport to your tailgate site.

The morning of your tailgate party, remove the roast from the refrigerator. Remove the roast from the marinade by placing it in a colander over a bowl to catch all of the marinade that drains off. Retain the remaining marinade in the double bags used to marinate the roast overnight. While the roast is draining, mix the remaining Dijon mustard and rosemary into a paste to coat the outside of the roast. You may want to make this paste the night before if you feel you will be hurried the morning of your tailgate party. Once the paste is made, rip off a sheet of heavy-duty aluminum foil about twice the size of your roast and lay the foil shiny side up on your counter. Spray the inner portion of the foil where the roast will touch the foil. Place the roast in the center of the foil. Coat the roast with the mustard and rosemary paste. Bring up the short edges of your sheet of foil and fold to seal the top into a seam. Fold both of the remaining edges to completely seal the roast. Repeat this process with a second sheet of foil, but this time put the foil on the counter shiny side down and place the foil-wrapped roast in the center of the foil. Do not spray with oil but continue the earlier process by folding the edges to seal the roast completely in a second foil wrapping.

Pour the bowl of drained marinade into the bag used to marinate the roast. Load your foil-wrapped roast and bag of marinade into your cooler if your transportation and equipment setup time takes longer than 1 hour. If not, feel free to transfer the roast and marinade in your picnic basket.

When you reach your tailgate location, set all of the appetizers out, equip everyone with their favorite drink, and light your grill using the indirect method. When the grill reaches medium-hot to hot, put the roast rack in the roast pan, coat both with cooking oil spray, and place on the grill. Add the roast, wrapped in foil, on the rack. Fill the roast pan under the rack with 2 cups of liquid. We use water or beer. Cover the grill and do not look at the roast for an hour.

After the roast has cooked for 30 minutes on the grill, get out your cookplate, saucepan, spoon, and bag of marinade. Light or start your cookplate, place the saucepan on the burner and pour in marinade. Bring to a moderate boil and simmer for the next 30 minutes.

Once the roast has cooked for an hour, uncover the grill and remove the foil from the roast. Pour any juice from the foil into the drip pan. Insert the meat thermometer into the thickest portion of the roast. Be careful not to insert the thermometer into an air pocket. If the pan is completely dry along with the foil wrapping, add 1 cup of water to the meat drippings. Put the cover back on the grill and cook for 15 minutes longer.

After cooking the roast the additional 15 minutes, check the meat thermometer. You will want to remove the roast from the grill at a 160-degree reading, so keep the grill covered and check often until the roast reaches this temperature. Usually a thermometer will move rapidly during the last 20 degrees of cooking. When you reach the internal temperature of 160 degrees, remove the drip pan, rack, and roast from the grill. Place the roast on the serving platter and cover with foil to keep it warm for the next 15 minutes. Add any drippings from the drip pan to the marinade simmering on the cookplate.

Announce that the tailgate dinner is almost ready and ask for a volunteer to carve the roast. While the roast is being sliced, turn the heat on the cookplate to high or medium-high so that the marinade comes to a full boil. While the marinade boils, mix 1 tablespoon cornstarch with 1/3 cup water in a paper or plastic cup. Mix thoroughly to eliminate all lumps, add to the marinade, and stir constantly. The marinade will thicken into a sauce. Reduce the heat on the cookplate to low and continue to stir frequently until the roast is cut and ready to be served. Remove the saucepan from the heat and place on the serving table next to the roast with a ladle for spooning the sauce over the pork roast.

SHASHLYK IZ BARANINY
(LAMB SHISH KEBAB)

This delightful entree will dazzle your guests, especially lamb enthusiasts. We first experienced this wonderful lamb dish while traveling in Russia. This version of shashlyk comes from the bourgeoisie. The Russian commoners make shashlyk with simpler ingredients: white wine or vinegar, bay leaf, lemon juice, pork, and onions. The traditional method of devouring the lamb is to eat it right off the skewer. We push the meat off the skewer into an aluminum foil pan so that tailgaters may easily dish up as much as they want. This recipe will generously serve six hungry tailgaters.

Ingredients

3 lbs boneless leg or shoulder of lamb, cut into 2-inch cubes, with all excess fat removed (I prefer leg over shoulder, but either will work.)
2 medium onions, cut into chunks
3 tablespoons freshly squeezed lemon juice
3/4 cup pomegranate juice
1/4 cup dry white wine
1/2 cup plus 2 to 3 tablespoons extra virgin olive oil
1 large onion, finely grated
1 tablespoon fresh cilantro or parsley, finely chopped
1 tablespoon fresh basil, finely chopped
1 teaspoon freshly ground black pepper
1 teaspoon salt
Cooking oil spray

Utensils and Equipment

Charcoal grill (preferably not gas)
Skewers (preferably long metal)
Jumbo-size plastic freezer bag
Wood (dry cherry or oak) or hickory chips
Grilling tongs
Basting brush
Premoistened napkins or towelettes
Large aluminum foil pan
Heavy-duty aluminum foil

Game Plan

The night before your tailgate party, cut two onions into eight parts by halving them horizontally, then slice into quarters. Prepare the marinade by mixing all of the following ingredients in a medium-sized bowl: lemon juice, pomegranate juice, wine, olive oil, onion, herbs, salt, and pepper.

Place the cubed meat and onion chunks in a plastic bag, either gallon or jumbo depending on the amount, and add the marinade to the bag. Put the bag in the refrigerator and turn over two or three times or as you think about it.

Gather the rest of your equipment together for easy packing the next morning. Do not forget the skewers.

The morning of the tailgate party, remove the lamb and onion mixture from the refrigerator and load in your cooler for transport to your tailgate location.

When you reach your tailgate location, set all of the appetizers out, equip everyone with their favorite drink, and light your grill employing the direct method, using the wood in addition to the charcoal. If you are using wood or hickory chips, start your charcoal fire and soak the hickory chips for 30 minutes in water.

While the coals are reaching the desired temperature, lift the lamb and onions out of the plastic bag and thread the pieces tightly together on the skewers. Retain the marinade in the plastic bag. Place the skewers in the aluminum pan and cover with heavy-duty aluminum foil until the fire is ready.

When the fire reaches medium-hot, spread the coals and wood. If you are using hickory or other wood chips, drain and sprinkle them on top of the hot coals, after spreading the coals. Spray the grill rack with cooking oil spray and place it on the grill. Heat the grill rack. Place the skewers on the grill rack. Brush with marinade. Turn the skewers occasionally and grill for about 15 minutes, continuing to baste with marinade. Line the aluminum pan with fresh heavy-duty aluminum foil. Remove the skewers from the grill after 15 to 20 minutes at most for rare to medium-rare lamb. Push the lamb and onions off the skewers into the foil-lined pan for serving. Announce to your fellow tailgaters that dinner is served. Cover the pan with heavy-duty aluminum foil to keep the seconds warm.

GRILLED JERK CHICKEN

For those of you who have had the opportunity to venture out to the perimeter of a Caribbean island, you have probably noticed the small straw huts along the roadside with a wonderful aroma creeping its way to your nose. This aroma is sometimes chicken, fish, or pork marinated and cooked in a pepper concoction called jerk. You will find bottles of this marinade in gourmet shops and sometimes grocery stores, which is much easier than trying to find all of the required exotic peppers. If you are not able to find the marinade, I have included two jerk sauce recipes. This recipe will feed six to eight. Make sure you have lots of Italian or French bread and butter to help control the spice in this entree. You will note that I recommend this for a cold game; the spice will keep your insides warm for the entire day.

Ingredients

2 frying chickens, cut into serving pieces
  or 4 breasts, 4 legs, and 4 thighs
1 bottle Jerk Rub or Marinade
Cooking oil spray

Utensils and Equipment

Kettle grill, gas or charcoal
Grilling tongs and brush
11 x 17 inch aluminum foil pan
Heavy-duty aluminum foil

Game Plan

The preparation for this dish is the same as that for Barbecued Ribs and/or Chicken, using the foil packet method. The difference is marinating the chicken in the jerk spice instead of the barbecue sauce. The amount of jerk marinade you use will depend on how spicy you like your chicken. Believe me, this dish is spicy, and most of the commercial marinades recommend that you use them sparingly. We joked the last time we cooked this at a tailgate that the marinade had already cooked the chicken before we put it on the grill!

The night before your tailgate, wash and pat the chicken dry. Set aside. Tear off a generous rectangle of heavy-duty aluminum foil. Lay the foil on your counter shiny side up. Spray generously with cooking oil spray the entire interior of the rectangle; edges do not need to be sprayed. Then drizzle jerk marinade on the foil and spread to cover a middle section where your meat will be placed.

Place your meat on top of the marinade. Depending on the type of chicken pieces you have, you may want to place the larger, denser parts, like the breasts, in a separate packet from the thighs and legs, since the latter cook faster. Separate packets allow you to place the packet with the smaller pieces on the edge of a hot fire for slower cooking.

Place your chicken skin side up. Once you have the chicken positioned on the foil, drizzle more sauce on top and spread. Now pull the short ends of your rectangle together to form a tent over the meat. With the two short edges together, fold tightly down to the chicken, folding the foil over and over in a fashion similar to folding a paper lunch bag. Once the short ends are folded, repeat the fold at the other two ends so that you end up with a sealed packet. Now repeat this process using another rectangle sheet of foil the same size as your first sheet, placing the foil on your counter shiny side down. Place your sealed packet in the foil, seamed or folded side down, and wrap again so that your packets have two layers of foil. Make sure your seals are tight and do not have any holes for the sauce to escape. If you have a problem with the sauce seeping out, wrap the package again with foil.

When you complete the wrapping process for all of the chicken you plan to grill, place the packets in your refrigerator overnight or, if you plan to grill the same day, refrigerate until 1 hour before you plan to grill when you will need to set the packets out to bring them to room temperature.

There is one last task the night before: make sure you set aside more jerk marinade for basting while you are grilling. Two additional cups of marinade should be adequate for the amount of meat listed above. If you are using the Jerk Rub recipe, bring more peanut or vegetable oil for basting. Be sure. to pack your grilling tongs, fork, and brush!

The morning of your tailgate party, load the foil packets in your car. There is no need to keep the chicken on ice since it needs to warm up a bit before grilling. A caveat to this rule: when it is a warm day and you do not plan to grill your fare for more than one hour after you remove the packets from the refrigerator, you will need to keep your chicken chilled.

When you reach your tailgate destination, set out all the appetizers, supply everyone with their favorite drinks, and light your grill using the direct method. Spray your grill rack with cooking oil spray and place it on the grill after you spread the hot coals. When the grill is medium-hot, place the packets on the grill, seam or fold side down, cover your grill with the lid, and leave it for 15 minutes. Turn the packets over and leave them for another 15 minutes.

After 30 to 35 minutes of cooking in the foil packets, unwrap your jerk entree. Pull the packets to the edge of your grill and, using your grilling fork, puncture each of the packets and tear the foil back. The foil will be filled with lots of juice so be careful while you pull the chicken out to place on the grill. Using tongs, place the chicken skin side up. Pour the juice from the packet over the chicken on the grill and cover with the lid for 5 to 8 minutes, depending how hot the fire is. Keep a watch to make sure your food does not burn. When you lift the cover, dab on more jerk marinade or oil and turn the chicken. Dab more marinade or oil on the side that is now up and cover the grill for another 5 to 8 minutes.

You may need to move your chicken around on the grill if some pieces are cooking faster than others. Your chicken should be done by now, but if it needs a bit more time, dab on more jerk marinade or oil and keep turning. Announce to all that dinner is served, remove the grilled entree to the 11 x 17 inch aluminum foil pan, and place the pan on your serving table.

Jerk Rub

If a commercial marinade or rub is not available, use either of the following jerk recipes. The rub is a simpler method.

Ingredients

2 tablespoons dried minced onion
4 teaspoons ground thyme
2 teaspoons ground allspice
1 tablespoon sugar
1 teaspoon cayenne pepper
1 tablespoon onion powder
2 teaspoons salt
1/2 teaspoon nutmeg
1/2 teaspoon cinnamon
2 teaspoons pepper
1 cup peanut or vegetable oil

Combine all of the spices in a mortar and grind them together with a pestle. Add 1/2 cup of peanut or vegetable oil to the spice mixture and combine to create a pasty liquid. Using your hands, rub the paste all over the chicken and wrap, using the foil packet method described above. Reserve the remaining oil for basting while grilling.

Jerk Marinade

Alternatively, the following marinade is probably closer to the real spicy concoction used by the roadside entrepreneurs in Jamaica.

Ingredients

6 scallions, green parts only, thinly sliced
2 large shallots, finely minced
3 large cloves garlic, finely minced or squeezed
1 tablespoon fresh ginger, minced or grated
1 teaspoon seeded, ribbed, and finely minced hot fresh
   chili (Scotch Bonnet or Habanero are preferred)
1 tablespoon ground allspice
1 teaspoon freshly ground black pepper
1/4 teaspoon cayenne pepper
1 teaspoon ground cinnamon
1/2 teaspoon ground nutmeg
1 tablespoon fresh thyme leaves or 1 teaspoon dried
1 teaspoon salt
1 tablespoon dark brown sugar
1/2 cup fresh orange juice
1/2 cup rice vinegar
1/4 cup red wine vinegar
1/4 cup soy sauce
1/4 cup olive oil

In a bowl, combine scallion greens, shallots, garlic, ginger, and chili. Reserve. In a mortar or another bowl, combine allspice, black pepper, cayenne, cinnamon, nutmeg, thyme, salt, and sugar. Blend by grinding with the pestle or mix thoroughly. Transfer spices to a bowl if you are blending with a mortar and pestle. Whisk in orange juice, vinegar, and soy sauce. Slowly drizzle in oil, whisking constantly. Add the reserved scallion mixture; stir to combine. Let rest for at least one hour. Marinate by rubbing the chicken with the sauce, using rubber gloves to protect your hands from the hot peppers. Wrap in heavy-duty aluminum foil as described above. Refrigerate until you pack the car the morning of your tailgate party. Continue the process by following the directions for grilling provided above.

CRUSHED BUCKEYE CHILI

This entree won Jim Brandstatter's Chili Contest at the 1993 Michigan vs. Ohio State game. Needless to say, the secret ingredient to this terrific chili is "crushed buckeyes." At least that is what I told Brandstatter, who loved the idea of the secret ingredient but also really loved the chili. This recipe is a rendition of Cincinnati 5-Way Chili published several years ago in the *Chicago Tribune*. I usually reduce the chili powder by half when we have tailgate participants who favor spicy but not fiery food. The winning chili recipe had the reduced amount of chili powder with half of the meat consisting of hot sausage. This recipe will generously serve six tailgaters.

Ingredients

1 lb ground chuck or 1/2 lb each ground chuck and hot
   sausage
1 medium onion, finely chopped
2 cloves garlic, minced or squeezed
1 cup barbeque sauce
1 cup water
1 tablespoon chili powder
1 teaspoon black pepper
1/2 oz unsweetened chocolate
1/2 teaspoon cumin
1/2 teaspoon turmeric
1/2 teaspoon allspice
1/2 teaspoon cinnamon
1/4 teaspoon ground cloves
1/4 teaspoon coriander
1/4 teaspoon cardamom
1 quart stewed tomatoes
16 oz canned kidney beans

Toppings

2 chopped spring onions
1 lb shredded cheddar cheese
1 to 2 pints sour cream, depending on how spicy you
    make the chili

Utensils and Equipment

Cookplate or cookstove
Large skillet or kettle with cover
Serving ladle or spoon

Game Plan

A night or two before your tailgate party, spray a large
skillet or kettle with cooking oil or coat with two tablespoons of olive oil and heat to medium. Sauté the ground
beef (and sausage if you are using it) with the onion and
garlic until browned. Drain the fat. Add the remaining
ingredients, except the kidney beans, and bring to a boil.
Cover and simmer at low heat for 30 minutes, stirring
occasionally. Remove the chili from the heat, let cool,
and store in the refrigerator overnight.

The morning of the tailgate party, place your pot of
chili back on the stove a good hour before you depart for
your tailgate location. Remove the chili from the refrigerator, place on a medium to medium-high burner and

add the kidney beans by stirring thoroughly. Reheat the chili by bringing it to a boil, then simmer, uncovered, for 30 to 45 minutes. Stir frequently to encourage thorough warming and check to make sure it isn't burning. Just before loading the car, wrap the chili in newspaper and load in a cooler or insulated container to maintain its heat. Alternatively, after wrapping in newspaper, wrap again in a blanket. Load it in your car along with the rest of the ingredients and equipment.

When you reach your tailgate location, immediately set up your tables and place your cookplate or stove at one end. Turn your heat source on medium to medium-low. Unwrap the pot of chili and set the pot on the cookplate or cookstove. Continue to warm the chili, again stirring occasionally to encourage even warming and prevent burning. Get out all of the appetizers and supply everyone with their favorite drink. Once it is hot, announce to all that the chili is ready. Place the bowls and toppings on the table near the pot. Ladle the chili into each bowl and have each tailgater add his or her desired combination of toppings.

INDEX

appetizers, 6
apples
　　baked, 8
　　shish kebab, 44
Barbecued Ribs and/or Chicken, 47
beans
　　baked, 70
　　chili, 87
beer, 38
beverages, 9
Blueberry Pancakes, 26
chicken
　　barbequed, 47
　　jerk, 80
　　Paella, 54
conversion process, 19
corned beef brisket, 66
Corn Kernel Pancakes, 27
Crushed Buckeye Chili, 87
desserts, 8
egg substitute, 26, 27
eggs, 31
equipment
　　cleaning supplies, 17
　　cooking devices, 16
　　cooking tools, 16
　　eating utensils, 17
　　processing containers, 16
fish/seafood
　　clams, 54
　　lobster, 54
　　mussels, 54
　　salmon, 60
　　shrimp, 6, 35, 54

ABOUT THE AUTHOR

Kathy Clyne Merrill is a graduate of the University of Michigan and has worked at General Motors for 19 years primarily in International Business, which has provided many travel opportunities to Japan, Korea, Germany, France, and Russia, among other countries. This has strengthened her love of gourmet cooking with a particular interest in replicating ethnic cuisine. A member of Rotary International, Merrill lives in Flushing, Michigan with her husband, Rick. With their friends and family, they spend many weekends tailgating during the University of Michigan football season.